Listening

Skills

Do You

REALLY

Hear

Me Now?

by

The Customer Service
Training Institute

Other Customer Service Training Manuals from The Customer Service Training Institute

Customer Service Basics

Conflict Resolution

Service Recovery Skills

How to Interact with All Kinds of Customers

Great Customer Service Over the Phone

Customer Service for Frontline Personnel

Enhancing the Customer Experience

Customer Service Training for
Service Technicians

Customer Service Training for
the Hospitality Sector

Customer Service Training for
Health Care Professionals

Customer Service Excellence for
Security Officers

Safety in the Workplace

Office Skills Training Series

Dealing with Difficult People

"If we truly hear what others are saying, the world & life just seems a little bit easier to understand.

Disclaimer

I hate these things as much as everyone else does but certain things just have to be said. This book is designed as an informative resource guide and is not intended to evaluate or identify any particular single situation. Every person and situation is different and some or all of the information in this publication may or may not be relevant to any individual or situation. It is the responsibility of the reader to understand the information and to decide what information is relevant and suitable for their needs. The publishers, writers and distributors of this book assume no liability for the use or application of any or all parts of this publication.

Table of Contents

Introduction

When it comes to misunderstood skills or activities, listening is way up there on the top of the list. The reality of it is that most people don't know how to listen. They haven't trained themselves to listen and they don't know how to listen.

When we think about communicating with people we usually think about talking. Which words we use, how clear we speak and how fast we talk. While all of those are important, we need to realize that no matter how clear or well we speak, if the person listening does not her what we say, everything is lost.

Failure to communicate properly is one of the major problems we have as a society today. People hear what they want to hear whether it is accurate or not. The result is misunderstanding, wasted time and a lot of wasted resources in the process. The only way to stop this is to make a serious effort to listen more effectively.

That is what this book is all about.

The great thing is that learning how to improve your listening abilities is one of the easiest things you will ever do.

It doesn't take a ton of time and you won't break a sweat any time in the process either! This book has over 10 great ways to improve your listening skills. (I know we said 10 but we just love to over deliver in our books!)

Now just because we list 10 things doesn't mean you have to learn all ten. You probably are doing a few already but even if you are I still hope you read through those chapters as well just so you understand why doing those things is so important. The book is not long and you should be able to read it in one or two evenings depending on how much time you have and what your attention span might be.

Just read it with an open mind and give everything a try. Don't dismiss anything straight off without at least trying it. Some people are astounded when they see how even the smallest change can produce big results!

You don't have to read the chapters in order because we write each chapter as a standalone topic. This means that some information may be repeated if it is relevant to more than one topic but the real importance stuff should be repeated anyway.

It's your choice, read it straight through or go directly to the parts that interest you the most. Whatever works for you is the best way to approach the book. But whatever you do don't rush through it. Read each chapter and spend a few minutes trying to see how you can use that information to increase your comprehension.

Everyone is different so what works for you might not work for someone else and vice versa. Figure out how to integrate some of these skills and processes in your life so you can boost your listening abilities.

Listening is a skill that few people really think about. They take it for granted but never really develop it. That's all about to change now………..

Listening Basics

Before we get started improving the way you listen to what is going on around you in life, we need to cover a few basics when it comes to listening. These may be things you already know but it is important that you understand them in the context of this book and what we are trying to accomplish.

First of all, there listening involves more than just hearing. You can hear something and not have it register in your mind. Background noises are a prime example of this. You hear them but our mind sort of just tunes them out and discards them. So you can hear without listening. Sounds strange but it's true.

You can also hear things that you don't understand. Hearing a sound that you don't recognize might be an example of this. You first hear it but it doesn't register in your mind. So then you take it to the next level and you "listen" to the sound. That means you not only hear it but actually listen for the tone and composition of the sound to try and figure out what the heck that sound really is.

So hearing is just picking up the sound but listening is paying attention to the sound and all of its meanings and components. So when you spouse says "Didn't you hear me?" you probably did but you weren't listening to them at that time. (I wouldn't advise admitting that, however, for obvious reasons!)

In this book, we are going to talk about listening skills. That means we are going to discuss not only how to hear something but also how to understand it and really get an accurate picture of what is being said and the content and emotions behind it.

Listening also involves more than just hearing. Listening also involves observation, emotion and retention. So I guess you can say that listening involves at least 4 basic parts. We need to physically hear the sounds, we need to understand what we have heard, we need to understand the emotions behind the words and we need to retain what we have heard. Failure to accomplish any of those 4 items can cause misunderstanding, misinterpretation and confusion.

Here is why each of those 4 parts is so important:

Hearing

This one is fairly obvious. If you can't hear the sound, you can't understand what is being said unless you can read lips or read closed captioning or some other visual aid. The ability to physically hear the sounds you want to listen to is the single most important part of the listening process.

After all, if you can't hear it in the first place there is nothing to understand or retain other than frustration.

There are many reasons why you might not be able to hear something. There might be too much background or environmental noise, the other person might not be talking loud or clear enough, or you might have issues with the quality of your own hearing. Whatever the causes might be, you should do your best to address them or make others aware so they can either talk louder or go somewhere that is quieter.

If the problem lies with your own ability to hear, then you should take steps to have that addressed. Hearing aids might offer you a cure for the inability to hear. On that same subject, everyone should have regular hearing checks especially as they grow older. Hearing can diminish with age especially when you were subjected to loud sounds earlier in life. Hearing tests are not expensive and they almost always are available locally.

Observation

Something a lot of people might not be aware of is the importance of observation to the listening process. Being able to see the source of what you are listening to not only makes it easier to understand what you are hearing, it also helps with retention and overall comprehension.

All our sense work together to help us understand and remember things.

So have a visual accounting of what was going on will also help use retain the content for longer periods of time. Seeing and understanding facial expressions, body language, outside environment and other things helps us to process the entire experience much more accurately.

In other words, listening means that we have to be aware of what is going on around us as well as what is being said in the conversation. Since outside influences also play a role in our ability to understand and remember, we need to make sure that we are aware of those things when they occur.

Emotion

Few people actually are aware of this but less than half of what we get from the communication process comes from the words we use. The rest of what we get from the communication process comes from emotion, visual clues such as expressions and body language and environmental clues.

The tone of the voice also indicates the emotions behind the words. From this we can usually get an idea of whether the person is angry or upset, happy or sad, or any number of emotional and physical states. In order to really hear the complete content of a conversation, you need to include everything. Being able to identify the emotion behind the words is important because it can give us clues so the urgency of something or the importance behind the conversation.

For example, if a family member or friend calls in a nice and calm voice and says "I need you to come over right now." You might think the situation was not critical and could wait. Or that even the reasons being given were not really true. But if that same person called up screaming in a panicked voice and said the same thing, you would be far more likely to rush right over or possibly even call for assistance at the same time.

In many cases, the emotions are even more important than the words.

Retention

Can we all agree that hearing something is not really all that important if we don't remember what we heard right after we heard it? I mean you can hear an important message, concentrate with all you might, get all the details and everything else but if you forget it all 3 seconds later the information is pretty much useless.

Memory sometimes is something that is designed into our DNA. I know some people who can remember every little thing for weeks and months. I also know other people who forgot what they had for breakfast by 10AM. While some people are just lazy and refuse to focus on their listening skills, others might have a legitimate problem when it comes to retention.

Really listening to something also means taking steps to make reasonable certain that you retain the information at least long enough to document it or use it.

For example, if your spouse asks you to pick up 4 items from the store on your way home, you need to remember that information only until you leave the store with those items. There is no need for you to retain that information for weeks and months.

But if you need to remember your password for your ATM card that is something you need to remember long term. There are different techniques for different situations and different applications. If you have a problem retaining information, it would be a good use of your time to investigate some of these techniques to help you remember information as long as you might need it.

One More Thing

There is one additional aspect of listening that we also need to discuss. It is more of a human brain type of issue rather than a hearing or listening issue. But it does play a role in how we listen and interpret and retain information.

That aspect of listening is "interest". In other words, you have to be interested in, or have an interest in what is being communicated to you. If you are not interested in what is being said, you will not be able to focus and you will lose interest and drift away.

Our minds tend to pay attention only when something is deemed as being interesting or if it fills a need in our minds. We will listen to someone explain how we can grab an advantage in our next job interview but we quickly tune out when someone tells us their new recipe for fried raccoons feet.

One topic has value to us and the other does not. (I apologize to anyone who enjoys fried raccoons feet!)

We have all found ourselves in situations where we quickly become bored with what is going on and our minds drift to thinking about what we have to do later, what is coming up for the weekend, or the big championship game that we have tickets for next week. That is because our minds find more pleasure and value in those things rather than what is happening now.

So one of the key aspects to listening and retaining information is to understand and create value and interest in that particular information so your brain will stay alert and focused. (By the way, this is not part of the Top 10 list. Consider this hint bonus material!)

Whatever we do when it comes to listening and hearing, we need to understand the differences between the two. You can hear without listening and you can listen without retaining. Neither one of those is particularly good. Those are the things we need to work on. And that's what this book is here to help you to do.

Words

As communicators, we often really get hung up on words. We choose them so carefully and we take pride in our vocabulary and our knowledge of the English language. But sometimes this gets in the way of actual communication. As far as communication is concerned, words are just one part of the process. And not one of the huge parts either.

I think of words as pieces to a puzzle. If you want to convey a thought or idea to someone else, you pick several words out of the box and string them together like assembling a puzzle. If all the words fit together properly, your thought will be communicated to the other person. If you choose the wrong words, or deliver them wrong, something else might occur.

We often get so caught up in words that we over complicate things. Most everything in life is better when it stays simple. Simple is good. The simpler something is, the more people can do it and do it well. And that's precisely what we are looking for when it comes to communication.

Our intention is to learn to communicate so that everyone can understand us. If we only can communicate using huge word with 15 syllables that only people with Doctorates can understand, then you are going to have an awfully hard time ordering a meal or buying a movie ticket. Our goal should not be sounding smart or impressing others with words. Our goal should always be successfully getting our points across to other people.

We will talk a great deal about why both people in a conversation have equal responsibility in the communication process. Both the person talking and the person listening are responsible for the success of the conversation. It is very important to understand this.

People should use words that most other people know when they speak. If someone hears a word they never heard before, they might not hear it right and become confused. Or they won't understand what the word means and they might be confused again. That's something we should try to avoid at all costs.

Here are two sentences. Which one is easier to understand?

"Is the interior ambient temperature in this domicile inherently less than the optimum required level for acceptable habitation?"

Or this one:

"Is it cold in here?"

Which sentence of the above would you think more people would understand and understand quickly? Obviously the second one. It is short and to the point. It uses words people are used to and quickly understand.

When we talk and when we ask questions, we should use common words that most of us quickly will know the definition of. For every moment someone has to think about what a word might mean, other words are being spoken and already have flown by.

So, in other words, get your point across with a minimum of complicated words.

For example, you are asked if you vote yes or no on a particular decision.

Here are two choices for your response:

"I hereby respond affirmative regarding the proposed matter being placed before me for a vote."

Or

"Yes"

People like short and sweet and a lot of people look at someone who insist on using long and complicated words and communicate in that fashion and annoying or downright obnoxious.

Another issue that complicates listening and communication is when people use technical language when talking to non technical people.

Most of the time non technical people will have no reason to recognize those words or term and therefore probably have no idea what they mean.

Would you understand this?

"By disrupting the current flow to the inverter we can reduce the output level of the generator's stator winding thus reducing the output to the load terminals until it reaches zero."

Or might this be just a little easier to understand?

"We just turn it off."

Same thought, same result, different words. Which would you rather have to listen to and understand?

So remember the next time you are listening to someone just how important it is to use the right words to convey your thoughts and ideas. Remember this when it comes you turn to respond to what you just heard. The words that you speak someone else has to listen to and interpret. When a shorter and easier word will do, use it. Whenever you have to use a longer or less familiar word, explain it.

Listening to normal conversations should not require a ton of effort to do. If it does, someone is doing something wrong. Don't let that someone be you.

Avoiding Distractions

Sometimes there are outside factors that keep us from absorbing all the information that is available to us. Sometimes those factors are within our control and sometimes they are out of our control. Either way, we need to address them to make it easier for us to really listen to what is going on around us.

Here are some common distractions most people encounter during a normal day:

Telephone

It is impossible to listen to someone when you are talking on the telephone to someone else. You cannot listen to two people at the same time and retain what both people have said.

If you are in a meeting, either as a leader or a participant, then leave word that you are not to be interrupted when someone calls. If the meeting is in your office, then mute the ringer or send the call to another location.

More time and information is lost during the day because of the telephone than almost anything else. It is a great tool but it can also cause a great amount of distraction.

To minimize or avoid this type of distraction, schedule important meetings or conversations to slower times of the day and arrange to have your calls held during these times. If that is not possible arrange for the conversation to be held in a quiet area where you are not in telephone contact.

Cell phone

This is something that has become an issue over the last two decades. It used to be that once you left the office you were immune to phone calls from co-workers, family, friends and other people. But with the fact that almost everyone has a cell phone, everyone is accessible 24 hours a day 6 days a week.

To make matter worse, your cell phone is not the only cell phone that can cause a distraction. People sitting or standing next to you that are talking on their phones can interfere with you hearing what the other person is saying. For this very reason many restaurants have instituted no cell phone policies and all movies, shows and concerts have this rule as well.

You simply cannot talk to people on the phone while listening to someone else talk and absorb and retain what everyone is saying. Even checking voice mail involves listening to someone else talk.

It also sends the wrong message to the other person speaking. Answering or making a call when someone else is speaking is like telling that person, "This phone call is more important to me than what you are saying."

Setting aside the effect this has on your listening, it is rude on your part and distracting to others.

Texting

The is the latest addition to telephone and cell phone use that provides a distraction and keeps people from absorbing everything they see and hear. In some ways texting is worse because it involves several activities at the same time.

When you talk on the phone you dial and once you are connected you simply talk and listen. Sometimes you only listen. But with texting you have to physically type in your message which takes time and thought. You have to pay attention to what you are doing and which keys you press. Plus, you have to read it to make sure it's correct and then hit the send key.

All of this time your eyes are off the person who is speaking so you lose the visual information. You are concentrating on what you are doing so you lose the verbal content as well. So you are distracted on multiple levels. This is why so many states and towns now ban texting while driving. This is because it requires more attention and provides a greater distraction than talking on your cell phone while driving.

Side Conversations

Whenever we are talking to someone else, even when not on the phone, we are dividing our attention between two or more sources.

So the guy sitting next to us at the seminar or in the meeting who likes to tell people about his last fishing trip is providing a healthy distraction for us at the same time.

Attending meetings or seminars or classes with friends and co-workers is sometimes counter-productive because you will be more likely to carry on private or additional conversations while the meeting or seminar is going on. While you are listening to the other person or talking, information from the teacher or speaker is passing you by.

Interruptions

I have held jobs where I worked in an office and others where I had a home office and therefore, worked in my home. Though I missed the human contact and interaction, I did realize that there were far fewer interruptions and many times I was able to eliminate unwanted interruptions when I wanted or needed to concentrate.

Whenever you are trying to listen to someone, be it a teacher, lecturer or just someone trying to carry on a conversation with you, any distraction will tear away your concentration and derail your train of thought. Even a short interruption could be enough to totally lose your place and wonder what it was you might have missed.

These interruptions might be phone calls, people just stopping by and sitting down in your office whether you want them to or not, or just every day office business that exists in normal offices.

Sometimes these interruptions can disrupt an entire day let alone one or two important conversations.

Multi-Tasking

I consider myself a very good multi-tasker. I can do several things at once and have several projects going on at the same time and get each one done. I can do e-mails and check spreadsheets at the same time and I can field phone calls and use my computer at the same time. Some people call it multi-tasking, others call it juggling and others call it just plain crazy!

But one thing I do notice is that whenever I do more than one thing at a time, one of those things is done sort of on auto-pilot. That means I do it almost without thinking. I do realize, however, that even when on auto-pilot my ability to get all the information that is going on around me is reduced. While sometimes this does not present a real problem, at other times it does.

I see people at meetings with their laptops open answering or sending e-mails, reading reports, or surfing the internet while the meeting is going on. I also see people in their phones or IPADS doing the same thing. Other are reading paperbacks concealed behind their laptops. Other people might have software programs open and they are either writing or creating something while the meeting is going on.

I don't care how good you are you simply cannot listen attentively and do creative projects at the same time. You also cannot craft responses to e-mails or create e-mails while retaining 100% of what someone is saying. At least I cannot do that.

Background noise

You cannot hope to understand what you cannot hear. Even if you manage to hear most of what is being said, you are bound to miss words and then have to attempt to "fill in the blanks" to replace those missing words. When this happens, a wrong word choice can totally change the meaning or intention of what was just said.

Sometimes conversations or communications in very noisy or crowded rooms are very difficult to understand. There are 47 different conversations going on at the same time and the words from one drift into the words of another and confusion starts.

Conversations should always be held in places that are fairly quiet and free from a lot of background noise. If you want to hold and extremely important conversation somewhere, hold it in an empty room far away from the mainstream activity. Don't hold it in the room next to the new construction where jackhammers and electric tools will add an unwanted dimension to your conversation.

The same could be said for high volume areas like concerts, ball parks, hockey arenas and such. Anywhere there are a lot of people talking, yelling or cheering is not the best place to try and understand what someone else is saying!

Other Obligations & Emotions

Sometimes we have a lot on our minds. We might have several things going on or problems at home. Maybe someone is seriously ill or having surgery and we are concerned about that. When this happens our ability to concentrate becomes impaired.

We can no longer keep our focus on the matter at hand and our minds drift back to our problems or issues. We sort of "tune out" on some things as our mind wanders in and out of the conversation.

While this is understandable at times, the person should be aware of this and either postpone the conversation or bring someone else into the meeting who can listen and process the content more completely and accurately.

Stress

Stress can keep us from listening well at times. Stress makes it more difficult to concentrate and keep a logical train of thought on track. Stress can also make us tired and lackluster. When we feel that way we find it more difficult to concentrate for more than a very short period of time.

Stress also causes disruption within our body which might make us feel tense or agitated. We might seem o edge or pre-occupied or just feel "down". This can lead to an inability to function at our best or to concentrate on anything for more than a few minutes or seconds.

Sensory Overload

Sometimes we will find ourselves in situations where there is just too much going on. Loud noises, congestion, people running all over, too many conversations or voices and a wide array of other things going on around us.

When this happens, or when we try and process too much information, we may go into a kind of mental overload where there is just too much to contend with. When this happens our brains just kind of shut down which is their way of saying "Enough Already!"

What Can You Do?

Distractions can bring havoc to a situation and there is little you can attempt to do except remove as many of these distractions as possible. Though your conditions might never be ideal, you can make your environment better to the point where you can hear and process information.

Here are some suggestions on how to reduce distractions

Block all phone calls, turn off ringers and place cell phone on mute. Better still; turn the cell phone on off. Vibrate is still a distraction.

Find a quiet location to have important or sensitive conversations if possible. This should be away from activity and preferably not have a phone.

Create a "quiet time" in your day to schedule important meetings.

Put a lock on your office or meeting room door and use a "Do Not Disturb" sign to reduce interruptions.

Implement a "no cell phones" policy at meetings.

Do the same for laptops. If laptops are needed for parts of the meeting they should be closed whenever not needed.

Have a "one person speaks at a time" policy whenever meeting in large groups. Not only is this respectful, it cuts the confusion level way down.

If outside distractions make it difficult to hear someone, let them know and ask them to speak up. Continuing to let someone talk when you can't hear them is futile.

Try to schedule meetings and conversations when you are calm. Never try and hold an important conversation when you are angry or upset.

Stop Talking!

There is a wealth of information available to us if we could just keep our mouths shut for a while so we could digest it. It is very hard to talk and listen at the same time. We need to step back and learn to let other people talk more and then process that information.

The human brain is an amazing structure and it is capable of doing many things at the same time. Unfortunately for us, it is already doing a lot of things even when we are doing nothing. It controls and regulates the entire body and everything that goes on inside of us. It monitors the various systems for warning signs that something is wrong and then it even goes and repairs itself when we get injured!

Then we go and add to the workload by moving, thinking, processing, dealing with our emotions and a host of other things we ask it to do every single day. So it is no mystery that our brains find ways of doing all these things at the same time. Unfortunately, sometimes the ways it comes up with are not as efficient as they should be.

Think about what goes on just with the process of talking. We rarely think about this because it is automatic with us just like breathing. We don't think about it because it has become habit. But just because something has become habit does not mean that you can do it without thinking. (Well, I do know some people who talk without thinking all the time but you get my drift!)

You have to think about what you want to say and then choose the words you want to use to convey that message. You have to control the mouth and tongue and lungs and vocal cords to produce those sounds and then you listen to them to make sure everything comes out as you wanted it to. All that time other people could be talking and while you would hear what they are saying, you don't really process it because you are busy doing other things.

While that is reason enough, there is another very important reason why you should stop talking and listen.

When people talk, they give us information. Granted there are a lot of times where people go on and on about something and just talk way too much. But even in those instances every once in a while a little bit of new information may come out that will help you or just make you aware of something you didn't know before.

When that happens you are able to make better and more informed decisions and your overall comprehension level can go up dramatically.

You are able to concentrate more, listen more and get more content. The combination of these factors makes listening a lot easier and more effective.

Talking when someone else is talking is not only rude, but it can be confusing as hell to other people. They try to process what both people are saying at the same time and trying to process the context and who said what when all at the same time. This can cause a LOT of comprehension issues for a lot of people.

Most of us talk too much as it is anyway. We usually can reduce the number of words we use and still communicate very effectively. In fact sometimes reducing the words we use can actually help our communication skills!

The more words we use the longer we talk. The more we talk the greater chances are that other people will get bored or tired of listening to us and they will tune us out. When that happens, those little bits of important information we just talked about can get missed. That can cause misunderstandings and confusion.

Here are a few things you can do to help yourself listen better and get more information:

Make an effort to talk less and listen more. It is sometimes just a decision you can make that will take care of everything all by itself. Be clear, concise and to the point.

Make sure people are finished with what they are saying before you respond.

Don't talk while others are talking. This is not only rude, but very confusing.

Limit or reduce the number of words we use when talking. Deliver the information but cut down on the time you take to deliver it.

Think before speaking. Ask yourself if your comment is worthwhile. In other words, don't talk just to hear yourself speak. If what you are saying has little or no value, it really doesn't need to be said.

Never interrupt someone (More on that later!) Wait a second or two after someone stops speaking to make sure they are finished with what they have to say before you respond.

Focus more on what the other person is saying and a little bit less on your response.

Remind yourself frequently that what the other person is saying is important to you. Even if it really isn't, tell yourself that it is. You never know what is going to be said and how it might help you!

Maintain Eye Contact
& Use Body Language

Very often people feel that they don't need to look at someone while they are speaking. They feel it is all right to look elsewhere, do other things, and not engage and be part of the conversation or process.

That is not a very good policy for several reasons. First, looking at the person who is speaking and making eye contact lets the person know you are paying attention and that you have an interest in what they are saying. This is important because when people see that the people or person they are talking to is interested, they will react and share more information.

When they see people looking down in their laps or at the floor or even sitting there with their eyes closed, they might be concerned that they are getting boring to listen to.

Even worse, they might feel that their message has little or no value. Add to that the fact that it is rude and disrespectful and you have a pretty good reason to make eye contact anyway.

Think about how you felt when you talked to someone and all you got was a blank look or the person was texting or reading e-mails while you were talking. Part of you felt insulted and you probably wanted to slam the laptop shut or throw the phone out the window. But another part of you probably questioned whether people were interested in what you had to say. If you felt that they weren't interested then you might cut your comments short and therefore withhold possibly important information.

You should always look at the person you are talking to. Make eye contact and use body language and movements to show you are engaged. Nod your head from time to time to indicate you are listening and agree with what is being said. Show that you are really listening and encourage the person to keep speaking.

Second, it lets people know that you are paying attention because your body is moving to face the person who is talking. If you were not paying attention, you would likely be staring elsewhere or just at one person while you mind was probably somewhere else.

The benefit to you is that you get to see what the person is seeing. You get to watch their expressions and watch their lips move.

Sometimes when you can't understand someone because they are not speaking clearly or because there are outside factors limiting your hearing, seeing the lips move allows you to figure out what word they were saying.

As we explained before listening actually involves more than your ears. You eyes pick up movements and your ability to observe allows you to look at someone and get a better idea of the emotions behind those words. If you see someone standing nice and relaxed you know he is comfortable in the situation and that's a good thing.

But if you notice the room is cool and the person is sweating up a storm, he is probably very nervous and sometimes that's a very good thing to know. If you notice someone is very red faced and animated, you might understand how mad the person is and that could change how you feel about the situation as well. Maybe the situation is more important or critical than you originally thought it was. Your eyes can often notice that.

Sometimes we also want to get an idea of the type of person we are talking to. Are they meek or aggressive? We they weak or strong? Are they self-confident or are they reserved? All of these things help us decide on the best response and the best course of action.

The other important factor, other than letting people know you are listening by looking at them, is that it shows you are engaged in the conversation.

This might lead to someone talking directly to you and making you the focal point of the conversation because they feel that at least you have some interest in what they are saying.

This can lead to you getting more information and even getting information especially relevant to you and you situation at the same time. This helps you gain an advantage over others at time and it also helps you make better and more accurate decisions.

You can get a lot of information from physical movements, body language and visual clues. Not to take advantage of this would be a mistake.

Do Not Just Hear Something, Experience It!

We just finished talking about stopping your talking so that you could concentrate and also about maintaining eye contact and acknowledging to the person speaking that you are engaged. This chapter is kind of an extension on that but to a far greater degree.

When we talk about listening skills, we refer to the ability hear the sounds, understand the sounds, determine their relevance and remember the information for as long as you need to. That is a lot to ask of two little ears and a brain that has a lot of other functions.

Fortunately for us our brains use other things to help them hear, interpret and remember things that occur in our lives. But for us to utilize all those things we need to do more than just listen to something, we need to experience it.

If you were to read a book, and then go see a movie exactly the same as the book, you would come out of the movie feeling differently about the story or the concept of the book. Not because the book was better or different than the book but because the movie, in addition to the words also gave you colors and scenery and emotion and many other things.

The same thing happens with listening as well. If you not only just listen to something but experience the entire event, you will understand and retail more of the information. But what exactly do we mean when we say "experience" the event?

By experience we mean using not just our ears but also all our other senses as well. We should see what is going on, look at the surroundings, notice what aromas are in the air and so forth. Anything that we can sense about the entire situation will help us understand and remember more.

Now I understand that if you are having a conversation with a co-worker, the environment might be the same and might not make any difference. But it still might be important if you need to recall details about the conversation.

Here's an example:

You are called in to provide details about a conversation that you had with another individual regarding a problem at work. Something that cost the company a lot of money. There is a question as to when this other individual was made aware of the issue.

He claims he was told at the end of the day after everything was finished. You thought you told him earlier in the day before things went wrong. Of course, he disputes this.

Had you had the conversation over the phone you might be able to check phone records but that's about it unless you can remember other parts of the experience.

But you remember when you were talking to this person about the problem you smelled really good smelling coffee from the store that brings in the Friday morning breakfast spread. You remember it because it smelled so good and you made a mental note to get some of that coffee before it was all gone.

Now smelling something might not sound like something important but in this case, if you remembered having the conversation when you smelled the coffee, that conversation must have happened sometime before 10 or 11AM because after that, everything would have been gone. So the other person's claim that he was not aware of the problem until late afternoon was false.

It is amazing how much we remember when we have different ways to recall information. We can recall sounds, smells, environmental factors, weather conditions, lighting levels and all of those things. Remembering these factors helps us piece together the other parts of the puzzle until everything makes sense.

Don't make the mistake of just listening to the words and ignoring everything else. We use all our senses every day in ways you might not be aware of.

Then, at a later date something is recalled that we didn't even realize and everything gets a lot clearer.

So now that we agree that it is smart to use all our sense when listening to someone, can we agree that it just makes sense to make a conscious effort to focus on doing just that?

Starting right now, let's make a pledge to start being aware of other things going on during a conversation. Start out with the things that might be a little bit strange or out of the norm. Those things often stick out from everything else and this would be an easy way to start.

Force yourself to notice the little things. Remember what the person was wearing, where the conversation took place, who was around at the time and anything else you might want to remember.

Memory and observation is like a muscle. If you use it, your ability to see and process more information increases. If you don't use it the ability will waste away. So starting right now, notice the little things. Don't just listen to something, really experience it!

Stay Focused & Alert

If you really want to retain and remember what you just listened to, your brain has to be engaged in the process. You cannot expect your brain to remember details of a conversation when your mind was otherwise occupied or your thoughts drifted off for a moment.

Some people have a habit of losing interest and getting bored fairly quickly. What had started out as an interesting conversation or lecture has now transitioned into boredom and restlessness. That could be because the process went on too long, the other person speaking was not interesting, or the topic held no interest for you in the first place.

If you and I were to go to a movie and it was an action movie with some of my favorite actors in it, I will have my eyes riveted to the screen and when it's over I will be able to tell people all about the movie. Maybe even share details that spoil it for them at the same time.

But when my wife and I go to one of her chick flicks, I often spend more time looking at my watch than watching the movie.

That's because I am interested in the action movie and am able to focus on it because it holds a kind of attraction for me. But the chick flick, well, that's something that I just wanted to be over because I found it boring.

The great thing about movies is that we choose to see the ones we want so keeping focused is much easier. We don't have that luxury at work or in our personal lives. We have to deal with certain situations. We have to do certain things even though we don't want to. In other words, we have to accept the good with the bad and be focused on both.

Sometimes that is a lot easier said than done.

When we are able to focus on something, we look more closely at everything. We become more engaged and we notice the little things that give us an added dimension to things. Everything looks clearer. Everything becomes easier to understand. Time also seems to go by faster when we are interested and focused.

When we become bored our focus goes in and out and we retain some information but not all of it. We miss out on certain things that were said or discussed while out mind drifted for a few moments. Things got confusing and harder to understand. Not because we became less intelligent but because we had less information to draw upon.

So the question people usually ask is "How can I focus more?" Well, here are a few tips on things you can do to help you become more focused and stay that way:

Know & Understand the Value in Something

If you are in a conversation or attending a lecture or class or just listening to someone for some reason, understand why you are there in the first place. Understand the benefit you are going to receive by being there and listening properly.

Are you going to learn something new? Are you going to learn something that will help you make an important decision? Are you going to learn something that will protect you or help you advance your career? Are you going to hear something that will help make you life better or easier?

If you can understand what you are getting out of it, your brain will take the benefits it will get and use that to keep you motivated and alert. No matter what anyone says, the "What's in it For Me?" attitude is a very powerful tool.

Participate

When we are in a situation where we have to listen to someone, we have a choice to make. We can either sit in the back and be invisible or we can become a participant in the conversation. We can ask questions, make comments and become an active part of the process.

When we make ourselves part of any process we almost automatically become engaged and more focused. After all, if you are going to ask questions or make comments, it really does help to pay attention to what is being said.

Otherwise you might come off looking like an idiot. I mean, you questions and comments need to be relevant and appropriate for what is being discussed.

If you are not focused and if you do not know what is going on, your comments could quickly expose you as someone who either is not very bright or not paying attention. Neither is a particularly good label to have associated with you.

Make It Relevant

We are pretty much a self-oriented species when it comes to what we do in life. If we see value in something we will pay attention to that and give it our best effort. But if we don't see the benefit for doing something, we will either push it aside or give it a sub-par effort. That is just human nature.

The problem lies in that everything is perceived differently from person to person. I might be interested in something for one reason while you might be interested in the same thing for entirely different reasons.

The key is to discover why something is important or relevant to you. Think about things you hear as "How will this help me?" "What in this conversation is going to help me in my situation?" If you can make something more relevant specifically in your life or situation, you will become more focused.

Another thing relevant topics do is help keep you alert because you are afraid that you might miss something important.

If the conversation or the topic is about solving a problem that you are involved in, your interest will increase and your alertness will increase at the same time.

Stay Awake!

Here are some tips designed to keep you awake and alert:

If possible, stand during conversations. It helps keep you from relaxing too much.

If you are in a meeting or a lecture, don't sit through breaks. Get up and stretch. Go outside if it's a little chilly out and revive yourself. Sitting all day will make you lethargic and you might actually fall asleep!

If you are holding the meeting, turn up the air conditioning and make it colder in the room. People in warm rooms tend to get drowsy more quickly. If you are a participant or student, ask the instructor to make the room a little colder.

Stretch and tense up muscles so your body doesn't get too relaxed and start to drift off.

Consider drinking a caffeinated beverage to wake you up.

For the same reason, avoid alcoholic drinks which not only can impair your ability to hear and process information but can also make you sleepy!

Follow the suggestions in the chapter about distractions so that you will have the best environment in which to listen.

Do Not Pre-Judge
or Jump to
Conclusions

One of the things that cause us to listen poorly and inaccurately is when we jump to conclusions or form our opinions too quickly or before all the information is received. Whenever this happens we stand a much greater chance of heading down the wrong path.

Very often we will be listening to someone and their situation or problem appears to be something we have encountered before. Maybe it is a customer with a particular product defect that is common or maybe a family member or friend that is telling you about a problem they are having with another person.

Sometimes when we hear something that sounds very familiar we think we know what is going on and we jump to conclusions. We don't really listen to anything more and already jump ahead to figuring out how we are going to handle this. Even worse, we might interrupt the person and tell them we know what their problem is.

We should never jump to conclusions no matter how certain we are of the situation or regardless of what the person is telling us. Once we do, we kind of shape everything we hear to fit our opinion or false conclusion. We don't hear facts, we hear what we think fits what we already decided.

So much of listening depends on what we are already thinking. If we keep an open mind, the information someone is providing us will be heard and used to shape an accurate opinion.

Think of listening and making decisions as a huge funnel. When you start you are at the top of the funnel where it is at its largest. This is at the beginning of the conversation when you are just starting to listen. The more you hear and the more information you gather, the more things that are eliminated and you move down further into the funnel. There are fewer possible choices or possibilities. Therefore there are fewer wrong choices.

As the person talks, and as you ask relevant questions, the more things get eliminated, the fewer possible choices there are and the further you move down the funnel. Finally, after the person is done speaking and you are finished asking questions, you are at the narrowest part of the funnel where you are very certain of what the proper course of action should be.

When we rush to judgment, or not let anyone finish what they are saying, we increase the risk of missing an important piece of information that might totally change the final decision.

This can mean delays, wasted time and resources, and escalation of tensions and bad feelings.

We will be talking more about questions and letting people talk a little bit later but for now, make an efforts to let the person keep talking until you feel you have all the information you can possibly get.

Don't rush the process and never try to short circuit the process and move on just for the sake of time. You probably will find that saving a minute or two in the information gathering stages will cost you a heck of a lot more later when you discover you made the wrong choice because you didn't get all the information.

Here are a few tips on how you can get the most information during a conversation:

Let the person speak and listen to their comments. Sometimes even when they are rambling on every once in a while something important will come across.

Ask open ended questions like "Is there anything else I should know?" or "What are your thoughts regarding this?"

When someone makes a general comment like "It starts making a funny noise" or "I don't like that" ask them questions to get more detail. Reply with something like "How long does it take before it starts making that noise?" or "What about this don't you like? Can you be more specific?"

Let the information guide your thoughts, not the other way around.

Encourage people to talk by acting and looking engaged in the conversation. If you look pre-occupied or bored, people might shut down and stop talking.

Make people feel comfortable when you speak with them. The more comfortable people are the more they talk and the more information you will get.

Continue to ask questions until you are fairly confident even if the person stops talking. Remember the funnel!

Do Not Interrupt!

Some people have a habit of interrupting people as they speak. Not only is this rude, it can stop, or at least inhibit, the free flow of information between the two people. When that happens, confusion and misunderstanding can result and emotions can get heated.

Some people hate getting interrupted when they speak and just about everyone reacts in a negative way when it happens to them. When you interrupt someone it is like you are telling them "What you are saying has little value to me. Be quiet and listen to me."

Though you are not really saying those words; that is how interruptions are sometimes interpreted. Naturally this will have a negative effect on your conversation. You might hear everything they say but if they're not talking, you're not listening.

Since it is important to keep people calm so accurate information can be exchanged without too much emotion behind it, it just makes sense not to do anything that will inflame emotions or make any situation or conversation worse.

Another vital part of the conversation process, one that we will talk about later in more detail, is that letting people talk allows them to vent their emotions and frustrations. Sometimes just the process of talking something out with someone is enough to calm them down so you can discuss things freely and without emotion or drama. You have heard the expression "I'm glad that I could get that off my chest." That is exactly what that refers to. People venting their feelings and emotions and feeling better just for being able to do that.

Interruptions also derail the other person's train of thought and they might forget what they are saying and important information can get lost. We want to have a smooth and constant flow of information so everything is revealed and everything is understood. We should always try to never do anything that interferes with the exchange of information.

Here are a few tips on how you can avoid interrupting people.

Wait for someone to stop speaking and then count to 2 or 3. If they don't start talking again, then you can speak.

Always listen to the tone and inflection of the voice and keep eye contact. This enables you to be more aware of when someone is done with their thought.

Do NOT ask them if they are finished speaking! This can be interpreted as an obnoxious or sarcastic comment and can get you in a lot of trouble.

Even if the person rambles on and on and loves to hear themselves talk, let them. You never know what you will hear and how it might help you.

Listening Aids

You might say that this chapter alone could be your Top 10 list all by itself. But sometimes no matter what we do or how hard we try, we need a little help in listening and retaining what we heard. Some of us are better than others when it comes to remembering and some of us have a lot more on our minds than others do as well.

With that in mind, here are a few ways you can help retain information longer and more accurately:

Use a Voice Recorder

Today you can buy small pocket recorders that fit in your pocket or go into your briefcase or just about anywhere. You can use these to record conversations or events so you can play it back later and transcribe it or just listen to it again.

This can come in handy when there is information that includes a lot of details and fine points. Or, when the information is delivered so quickly that you can hear it but not process it.

If anyone has seen their favorite comedian at a show you often realize you laughed so hard during the show but can only remember a handful of the jokes afterwards. That is because they were delivered rapid fire one after the other.

Now we should stop right here and let you know that some seminars or public events do not allow recording and you can get into some serious trouble if you attempt to record the speaker for any reason. So always be upfront and if there is any question whatsoever about what you are allowed to do, ask. The penalties can be severe.

The same goes for recording private or business conversations. It is usually against the law to record a conversation when others are unaware that they are being recorded. This applies to both face to face conversations as well as phone conversations. You should always make everyone involved aware that the conversation or meeting is being recorded.

Take Notes

One of the best ways to remember something is to write it down. If you think about it writing something down actually makes you think about the information 3 times. The first time is when you first hear it. The second time is when you write it down. The third time is when you read what you wrote.

So there are 3 instances where you brain becomes engaged I what you are doing. This is one of the best ways to learn now things.

Writing things down also helps you remember and document information that is more important to your own situation and needs. You might attend a 6 hours seminar and come away with just one page of notes about just 3 topics. But if that information is very relevant and useful to you, then making sure you have it all down on paper so you remember the fine points is a great way to remember important information.

Paraphrase

Paraphrasing is when you take something someone says and then restate it in your own words. For example, if someone says "The use of technology today has enabled the business world to accomplish much more in shorter periods of time thus increasing efficiency and productivity." You can turn that into your own words and write down "Technology and computers have allowed businesses to do more in less time."

The meaning is the same but the words are different. But think about how effective this method really is. In order to put something in your own words, you have to understand it in the first place! You cannot re-state something in different words if you don't know what someone was talking about!

You can also restate things during the meeting or the seminar to make sure you have the right message and understanding. For example, you could say during a seminar "So, let me make sure I understand this.

What you are saying is that technology has helped businesses do more in less time. Is that correct?" Or during a meeting, you might say "So what I'm hearing is that the Simmons project is going to come in under budget but will take a bit longer to complete. Is that correct?"

Every time we restate something in our words it involves understanding and thinking about it in more detail. Comprehension and retention go hand in hand. The more you think about something the more you understand it and the more likely you will be to retain it.

Use Association

It is almost always easier and more effective to remember something in the terms of how and why it is relevant to you. If you can attach a personal benefit to something it is like giving that idea life and purpose.

You might sit in a meeting or at a seminar and hear someone talk about 35 different things. But if something has a purpose in your life or situation, your ears will perk up and you will focus more on what they are saying.

When you are listening to someone, try and attach some personal significance or benefit to that information. Try to put it in terms of how it is going to help you. If you can do that, you are far more likely to remember it.

For example, if you attend a seminar and the instructor says "After market surveys have been shown to improve customer satisfaction an average of 13%" that is good information and you might remember it. Or you might not.

But if you said to yourself "If we use after market surveys we could see a 13% improvement in customer satisfaction which would help us meet our goals and increase business next year!" you would likely stand a better chance of remembering everything in more detail.

Our brains attach more importance to things they see will provide us with a benefit of some kind. If something is perceived as positive and has potential make your life better, easier, or more rewarding your brain will listen. If the same information is viewed as generic in nature, you might just ignore it and miss out on something of great value.

So if you can, take information you hear and make it personal.

Talk to Others – Compare Notes

Sometimes it can help to compare notes and discuss things with other people. If you go to a seminar, perhaps discuss things with others at breaks or during lunch. Getting a different view on something makes you think and thinking about something helps you remember it.

Another reason to discuss things with others is that sometimes they will pick up on something that you missed. Or they will have a use or application for that information that you never thought of. That is why seminars are good ways to learn about new things. Not so much because of what the instructor might say but how the students react to it.

Use the Information!

But always keep in mind any time you talk about something or discuss something you are making the memory stronger and are likely to retain it longer. Every time you refer back to that information you are telling your brain that this information is important and that tells you brain to remember it better and longer.

That is why things we use every day we remember. Your password that you use to log into your voice mail you will remember. But if you are out sick for a long time, you might forget it. The same thing for your ATM password.

But try and remember your locker combination from Junior High school. At one time you could remember it easily because you used it several times a day. Now, even if I offered you $1,000 I doubt if you could recall it! Things we use everyday are the things we remember best.

Asking Questions

Part of listening involves understand what we heard. The best way to do that is by becoming an active part of the conversation and asking questions to make things clearer. Asking questions makes you think about what you just heard so that you can know what questions to ask.

You would be surprised how many people will go through a conversation, or attend a meeting and not really know what is going on. Yet they fail to ask a question to help clear up any confusion and avoid any misunderstanding.

If you stop and think for a moment, doesn't it make sense to ask questions NOW when the subject is being discussed and when people who know about the subject are there right in front of you? Some people feel that asking questions makes them appear stupid but the reality is that the exact opposite is true. When people don't ask questions and when they make mistakes because they don't understand what they were listening to that they look foolish.

Asking questions increases your engagement in the conversation and that also increases awareness and focus. When you are more focused and more engaged, you listen better, you understand better and you just remember things better and more accurately.

Asking a question might lead the other person to explain things a little bit differently or be a little more specific about something to make it easier to understand. The important thing to remember, especially when you are part of a larger group, is that the same thing you are thinking about asking is something that someone else is probably wondering about as well. So no one is going to think you are foolish or stupid for asking the question. Quite the contrary, they will appreciate that you asked so they didn't have to!

This is pretty self explanatory and should require nothing else but just to be sure; here are some suggestions on how you can use questions to improve your listening skills:

If you don't understand something, stop the conversation and ask for clarification.

Ask that something be explained another way so that you can better understand.

Ask open ended questions to encourage more detail and more information.

Ask specific questions to make specific items clearer to you.

Find out how you can contact the other party at a later date if any questions should come up.

If relevant, give an example and ask how this particular information might help you. (Making things more personally relevant.)

Unless specifically requested, do not wait until question and answer periods to ask your questions. Ask them at the point where you begin to not understand what they are talking about. Waiting until later might cause you to get too far behind or even result in you forgetting your question when the time comes.

Write down questions you might have if you are asked to hold questions until the question and answer segment. This will help you remember which things you wanted help on. As time goes by if you start to understand, you can always cross the question off the list. Or, if someone else asks it first, you can cross it off the list as well.

Be Calm and Stay Calm

The best way to listen to something or someone is to do it when you are calm. Whenever anger or frustration enters the picture emotions can take over and distort your interpretation over what you hear. It is very difficult to exchange accurate information when one or both parties are angry of upset.

Have you ever tried to talk to someone when they were really angry? When anger and yelling form the majority of the conversation? When this happens more effort is spent trying to separate the emotion from the words than trying to understand the words themselves.

Three things happen when someone is angry and you try to communicate with them. They tend to exaggerate things and they tend to block out anything you say that is not exactly what they want to hear. They also tend to speak faster than normal and this alone can make it more difficult to understand what they are saying. The combination of these three things makes positive communication almost impossible.

When people exaggerate things, it makes you wonder which things are exaggerated and which things are really true. When someone says "This damned thing has been breaking down every week for the last 6 years and I've had it!" you pretty much know it has been breaking down but the every week for 6 years is just not reasonable. No one would put up with something that long.

The best strategy for communicating with an angry or upset person is to spend your initial efforts trying to get them to calm down. Reassure them that the reason you are here is to help them. Let them know what has happened in the past is in the past and right now you are committed to helping them.

Show empathy for their situation. Don't tell them you understand as that usually just makes people even madder. Don't accept responsibility for the problem either if you shouldn't because that can come back to haunt you later as well. Instead, tell them you are sorry that this has become the problem that it has and ask them to let you help them resolve the problem. At this point all we want to do is calm the person down.

We should also try to avoid the use of negative words such as can't, won't, will not, no, and other words that usually mean the other person is not going to get what they want.

For example, if you reply to a demand is "I'm not allowed to do that but I can give you a complete refund, give you a replacement product and pay to have someone wash your car and mow your lawn for the next 10 years." All they hear is "I'm not allowed to do that."

Now some of you reading this are thinking, "What the heck does this have to do with listening skills?" Well, in order for you to hear and listen, people have to be talking and communicating with you. If they are not doing that in such a way that you can understand, then that becomes a listening issue.

Remember when we stated that the communication process is the responsibility of everyone involved in the conversation or situation. Both have to speak and listen and understand for the process to work. If only one person tries, both people usually fail. That might not be fair but it is the reality.

That other thing that happens when people are angry or frustrated is that rational thought and reasoning usually go on vacation. When this happens reasonable resolutions or questions are dismissed or misinterpreted and confusion starts and anger and frustration build. This just makes things worse and then the entire situation can spiral out of control.

So your first responsibility is to keep yourself calm despite how the other person treats you. That sometimes is easier said than done but you really need to make every effort to stay calm.

That is because it is much harder to continue to yell at someone who is calm and nice. It is also hard to stay angry at someone who is calm and smiling back to you.

Your second role in the beginning is to bring the other person closer to a calm state of mind. Once you do this then you can start to find out the truth behind things without the anger and exaggeration. Knowing accurate information helps you make better decisions and more accurate resolutions.

To better help you stay calm and help get others to calm down as well, consider doing some of the following:

Don't take things personally. Most of the time anger is directed at the problem not the individual. Even if it is directed at you, it is most likely directed at your position or your role with the company or your relationship with someone else, and not at you as a person. Even if it is directed at you personally, don't take it to heart.

Keep calm and smile even when you are being yelled at.

Give the other person their person space. Do not get into someone's face or get too close.

Never get confrontational as a response to the other person getting confrontational. This never ends well.

Always try to be a calming influence

Make all statements from a positive point of view telling people what you can do and not what you can't.

Try and separate the emotions from the words to get as accurate a picture of what's going on as possible.

Always reinforce to the other person that you are here to help resolve the situation and not to ignore it or make it worse.

Be empathetic whenever possible.

If you cannot calm the other person down, possibly find someone else you can escalate the issue to. Sometimes this is all that the other person is looking for.

If you try to calm someone down but just can't, consider asking if you can carry on this conversation at a later time when everyone has calmed down a bit. Sometimes this snaps people out of their rage when they realize it is being counter-productive.

Let the other person talk and vent. This usually helps calm people down. It might take a while, but it usually works well.

Always direct your efforts on things that will make the conversation and situation better and calmer. Never fan the flames of anger or respond in an angry manner.

Be Patient – Let People Talk

One of the very best tools you can use to improve your listening skills is to develop the patience to just let people talk. Letting people talk accomplishes several things that result in you understanding more and preparing yourself to make better and more accurate decisions. At the same time you are allowing the other person to explain their position, vent their frustration and voice their concerns.

Very often we are more concerned with getting things done quickly and don't focus on the value in letting people express ALL of their feeling and share ALL of their information. We tend to steer the other person in the direction we feel the conversation should or we jump to conclusions based on a small bit of information that we heard early on in the conversation. Both of those tenancies can be very dangerous for all concerned.

Some people take a long time to talk. They use a lot more words than they really need to and sometimes get so caught up in minute details that is seems to take forever for them to get to the point. This can be very frustrating to the listener but it is important to understand that we need to keep the flow of information moving smoothly and we should not do anything to interrupt or disturb that flow.

People have a method of getting from one point to another. For some of us we prefer to be direct and straight to the point. No messing around just straight to the facts. Others like to share back stories and other information which might not even be relevant to the topic being discussed. But for some reason, it seems relevant to them so we need to allow them the time they need to fully tell their side and express their opinions.

Letting people talk also has a calming influence as well which can come in very handy when you are listening to an angry or frustrated person. Just the act of telling you their story can calm people down. They want someone to listen and share their pain and understand what they are going through. For better or worse YOU are that person and you need to listen to them.

I was employed in the service industry for most of my career and you wouldn't believe the long winded stories we would get from people who were angry that their product had broken.

We would listen to story after story about this and that but every once in a while one of the stories would contain a little tidbit of information that changed the way we looked at the situation. Something that appeared to the other person as irrelevant was suddenly part of the decision process and caused us to go in a completely new and better direction. Had we just this person down, we might have made the wrong decision and wasted time and money going down a path that we shouldn't have been going at all!

As far as the other person is concerned, people who take the time and listen to them appear to be more interested in helping them. While that might not actually be the case, it is their perception and perception is very important at times. If you take the time and make the other person feel that you care about them and their issue, you stand a much greater chance of getting them into a more cooperative mood later on.

Now this doesn't mean we have to stand by for an hour and a half while a co-worker has to explain why a late night meeting annoyed his wife who was having a visit with her Aunt Shirley who has the gout and had to be taken to the hospital for the same thing in 1985.

When the other person gets too far off track, instead of stopping them, ask them a question designed to get them back on track. For example, say something like "Now you said the client got upset when you first brought up the fact that the budget was going to be an issue."

This will usually get things on track in a gentle manner.

Another reason for allowing people to talk is that as long as they are an active part of the process they will continue to share information with you. As long as they are sharing information with you, the process can move on. But when they shut down, the process can come to a screeching halt.

Always remember that listening is just part of the communication process. Your ability to listen correctly and keep the process moving is one of the most important parts of listening. Allowing people to talk and vent and share information is a critical part of that process.

Here are a few ways you can help people share more information:

Act interested and engaged. Don't make people think they are talking to the wall.

Ask people questions that show them you really are listening.

Make it clear that you want to help resolve the issue not ignore it or prolong it.

Make everyone feel that they are part of the process and not just bystanders.

When people start to ramble off topic, ask questions designed to get people back on track.

Never interrupt when people are trying to vent their frustrations.

Take a Break!

Like everything else in life, there is a limit on how long we can focus on a specific task or situation. When that amount of time is exceeded, we perform at a lower level and the results we produce decrease.

Have you even been in a meeting that went on and on for hours? Did you find yourself "zoning out" or day dreaming? Most of us can only concentrate effectively for a certain period of time. After that, we no longer retain information or pay close attention. That is why seminars and meeting often have breaks.

The breaks are there not only to allow people to go to the bathroom or stretch their legs. They are also there to allow the brain a little down time to recover and start to refocus. It doesn't take that long but the breaks are necessary.

The same goes for listening to conversations or explanations. If the process gets to be too long, your ability to maintain adequate concentration decreases. This means important information might be missed or not properly understood. This can lead to confusion and mistakes down the road.

Because of this it is advisable to monitor how long something has been going on and take frequent breaks so people can refresh themselves before continuing. It is well worth the 15 or 20 minutes to allow people to take breaks. Very few people can go for hours on end without a break.

We also need to consider that other demands on a person's time might be too much for them to engage in long meetings with you or anyone else. You cannot expect someone with huge workload to sit in a 7 hours meeting while things pile up in his inbox. He might be sitting in the meeting but his head is thinking about how much stuff he is missing and will have to catch up on. Needless to say, that person's concentration level will be lacking.

So allowing people to go too long without breaks is more counter-productive than anything else. With that in mind, here are a few things you can do to make sure you, and everyone else, is able to remain focused and able to communicate clearly and effectively:

Schedule multiple short meetings rather than one large one.

Make an effort to take frequent breaks.

Take a break when you notice people losing focus or yawning.

Take a break when you see people doing other things like checking their cell phones, opening their laptops or texting. This is a sure sign of loss of interest.

If you see tempers starting to flare up, take a break to let people calm down a bit.

If it is near the end of the day, consider picking things up tomorrow.

Be aware of the schedules and responsibilities of the other people involved and try to schedule around them to minimize things. People will appreciate this more and be more willing to give their time and cooperation.

If this is a scheduled meeting or seminar, make break times known in advance so people can plan them into their day. For example if an important phone call must be made, it can be scheduled for a break so it will not be delayed.

Don't try and jam too much content or topics into one meeting. If it goes on too long people will zone out.

If you find yourself day dreaming or losing focus, get up and walk around or stand in the back of the room. Sometimes this will allow you to wake up a little.

If there are refreshments in the room, stand up and go get a cup of coffee or a cup of soda. Caffeine can help give your system a little jolt to wake you up.

If the meeting is held in winter, or if it is chilly outside, walk outside for a minute. The cold air can wake you up and refresh you. Do this during breaks so you don't miss any content!

How Is Your Hearing?

No matter how hard we try or how much we concentrate, if you don't have the physical ability to hear well, all your efforts might prove futile. A large number of people today experience some form of hearing loss. This hearing loss can make it difficult, sometimes impossible, to function properly in all aspects of life.

Imagine not being able to hear a waitress ask you questions about your food order or hear the instructions being given to you by your boss. Or having your significant other whisper special things to you only you can't hear them.

This is the life that many people lead who experience partial hearing loss. That is why it is so important to take steps to protect the quality of your hearing or to take action if you already have experienced some hearing loss.

Hearing sometimes decreases as we get older. This change is so gradual you might not even notice the changes. It's not the same as realizing things look fuzzy and that you might need glasses. Instead, other people sometimes realize you have hearing problems before you do!

Everyone should have their hearing tested when they are younger to establish a base line for future tests to be measured against. This lets the doctor see how much, if any at all, hearing you lost over a specific period of time. It also helps identify any genetic hearing issues that might already exist.

The test should be repeated as you get older. Ask your doctor when a hearing test should be done. Naturally, if you have some kind of hearing loss, follow-up testing should be done more frequently to monitor the progression of the loss.

Fortunately for those who do have some level of hearing loss, there are devices that can help you. There are various types of hearing aids that you wear, there are telephones with higher volume features and there are even some pocket amplifiers you can stick in your pocket that amplify surrounding sounds,

If you are aware of any hearing loss, or if things do not sound clear and easy to understand, perhaps you do have some kind of hearing loss. If people sound like they are mumbling, or you have problems understand when someone talks to you, these are the signs of possible hearing loss.

When you find yourself with the warning signs, seek help immediately as the longer you go without attending to the problem the worse your hearing can get. See a doctor and schedule a hearing test. They will give you their evaluation and suggest an appropriate plan of action which may or may not include hearing aids.

Today's hearing aids are relatively discreet which means they are not bulky or very obvious. There are some that are practically invisible. Don't refuse to get a hearing aid because you are ashamed or be afraid people will make fun of you. Today people understand situations like this and are far more informed than they used to be.

There usually is no good reason why you should have to suffer with hearing loss today. Take advantage of the technology available to us today to restore your hearing and your ability to listen, hear and understand what goes on around you.

This is more than hearing conversations or directions from your boss. It is also hearing your children laugh and play, your spouse telling you that they love you or just hearing the everyday sounds that we used to take for granted. You should not deny yourself those sounds if you don't have to. Have your hearing checked by a qualified professional today.

If your hearing is a little lower than normal but not bad enough for a hearing aid, here are some things that can help you. Even if you do wear hearings aid, these tips will also help you as well.

Turn to face the source of the sounds. You will understand and process more when you can look at the person speaking.

If someone calls you from across the room, move closer to them so their voices are louder.

Try and keep your environment as quiet as possible.

One of the common signs of hearing loss is the inability to hear well when there are backgrounds noises present.

If you know that someone has hearing problems, don't talk to them when you are standing behind them. Get out in front so they can see you.

One indication that someone has a hearing issue is if they talk louder than normal. It makes sense that if they cannot hear you, they have the same problem with hearing their own voice.

Since most mild hearing loss deals with clarity and certain types of sounds, it can help to turn up the volume on the television or the telephone. As far as people are concerned, ask them to speak up a bit.

Some people tend to have very soft voices and they speak very low to the point where even people with normal hearing might have trouble understand them. It might be worth it to nicely tell that person that they are speaking too low and you can't hear them.

If you notice you have trouble hearing, tell family members and close friends about it so they are aware. This is nothing to be embarrassed about. But if others are aware, they can make an effort to talk a little louder to you or make sure to stay in your line of sight while talking with you. It's these little things that can make a big difference in your overall quality of life.

People with hearing loss may hear things but have trouble with the clarity.

Certain soft sounds tend to get lost and one word can sound like a totally different word. This can cause confusion and mistakes. If you experience this type of problem then you really need to make an effort to maintain eye contact and keep distractions to a minimum.

If you need hearing aids, get them.

If you have hearing aids, wear them. Your hearing will sometimes get worse much more rapidly if you refuse to wear your hearing aids.

If your hearing is good, following these suggestions will help keep it that way:

Avoid loud noises or sounds. These can damage the lining of the ear and lead to future hearing loss.

Wear ear plugs or hearing protectors when using loud equipment or going to concerts.

Turn down the level of music when using ear buds. They actually stick into the ear canal and loud music can damage the ear.

Consider using over the ear headphones instead of ear buds. They are bulkier but they are better for protecting your hearing. Even with the over the ear models, keep the level down.

Wear headphones or wear hearing protection when using lawn mowers or chain saws or other very noisy tools.

Cover your ears if you know a very loud noise is about to happen.

If you have any kind of ear infection, discharge of fluid from the ear, ear ache or any problem with your ears, don't wait and see if it will go away. Get to a medical professional as quickly as you can. Some ear problems can cause lifelong hearing problems.

Conclusion

It's important that we understand and agree that communication is the responsibility of everyone involved. If someone is talking but no one is listening, we have failure. If everyone is listening but the person talking cannot be heard or understood, we also have a failure. It is only when people are talking correctly and heard properly that communication can be effective and considered a success.

For most of us reading this book, I think it will just be a little change of attitude that is all that will be needed. Often just being made aware of something is all that is needed to make a considerable amount of change.

If we understand that we are an integral part of all communications, we will likely give it greater attention and attachment greater importance to it. Once we accomplish that, many other things just happen by themselves.

But just in case that you are one of those folks where stuff doesn't just happen, I hope you will read this book from cover to cover and give some thought to how you can use this materials to improve your listening skills.

Take the content and make it relevant to you. Take each tip or idea and figure out how to integrate that into your life or your situation. Once you make things more relevant and more personal, you will have more success in whatever you do.

But if you already read this book, you would know that.

If you would like some more information about Listening Skills or other similar topics, please visit our website at:

http://www.infowhse.com

for more information. Be sure to sign up for our newsletter which will give you other FREE information as well as another FREE E-Book!